The Bulu Line

Also by Stuart Cooke

Poetry
Edge Music (2011)

Criticism
Speaking the Earth's Languages:
A Theory for Australian-Chilean Postcolonial Poetics (2013)

George Dyuŋgayan's

Bulu Line

A West Kimberley Song Cycle

transcription and gloss by Ray Keogh
with Paddy Roe and Butcher Joe Nangan

Edited and Translated by Stuart Cooke

PUNCHER & WATTMANN

First published in 2014
Published by Puncher & Wattmann
PO Box 441
Glebe NSW 2037

http://www.puncherandwattmann.com
puncherandwattmann@bigpond.com

National Library of Australia
Cataloguing-in-Publication entry:

Dyuŋgayan, George
The Bulu Line
ISBN   9781922186539

I. Title.

A821.3

Cover Design by Matthew Holt

This project has been assisted by the Australian Government through the Australia Council, its arts funding and advisory body.

Australian Government

Australia Council
for the Arts

Contents

Acknowledgements

I first encountered Ray Keogh when I read *Reading the Country*, but then I came across his doctoral thesis while I was doing research for my own.

Stephen Muecke was one of my supervisors, and I'd decided to follow up the books that Stephen had written about Broome and surrounding Goolarabooloo country. After my first trip there, back in September of 2007, I couldn't forget the place. Broome's colours, textures and histories infused my poetry and prose and, even though I was on the other side of the continent, I knew that I'd end up writing about the place for many years to come. A few visits and lots of poems later, I'm extremely privileged to have been shown some of Goolarabooloo and Yawuru country by men as knowledgeable as Richard Hunter, Joseph Roe and Franz Hoogland, and to have received invaluable help from some associated whitefellas like Deborah Vincent and Stephen.

Alongside these visits, and present at some level in all of my associated writing from this time, has been Keogh's pioneering analysis and explication of *nurlu* songpoetry. If Stephen Muecke showed me how to start reading the West Kimberley, then Ray Keogh taught me something of how to listen to it.

For this book, I have to thank Stephen most of all, for without his initial encouragement, and without his ferrying of manuscripts and permissions forms between Sydney and Broome, this project might never have been completed. I am indebted to Kim Ackerman as well, who patiently went through this manuscript with a fine-toothed comb, and enhanced it beyond measure with his expertise and insight. My heartfelt thanks also go to Deborah Bird Rose, for guiding me towards country in the first place, and to David Musgrave, for supporting *Bulu*'s publication.

Finally, I would like to thank Anne Keogh, for kindly allowing me to use Ray's thesis as the basis for this book, and Phillip Roe, for giving his permission to publish the *Bulu* translations. *The Bulu Line* is indebted to the generosity and support of each of these people.

Preface

I cannot over-emphasise the importance of this kind of work. Australians are only too familiar with the significance and value of Indigenous arts as part of the national heritage and of the contemporary repertoire. We are familiar, but they still take us by surprise. In the late 1970s, those who had the habit of mourning cultural loss in the central desert, suddenly witnessed the flourishing—like desert flowers after rain—of an art movement that critic Robert Hughes dubbed 'the last great art movement of the 20th century'. But when we compare it to the oral traditions of the continent, we have to marvel at the ease with which that visual art was translated from ochres into acrylics, then translated into art-commodities and transported to eagerly awaiting patrons around the world.

Compared to that art movement, the song and poetry traditions seem to be sadly languishing. Who has the expertise to accomplish the tasks of linguistic translation? Thoroughly bilingual poets are extremely rare. Poets and storytellers in traditional Australian languages have yet to be fêted on the literary festival circuits. Yet despite the disappearance of many languages, we should be wary of announcing the demise of these literary traditions too early. They have that power held by sustained longevity that could emerge again, like those desert flowers, and we can never be sure what form they will take.

This is why I stress the importance of this kind of work. It is conscious of the weight and importance of all those oral traditions in the continent; the 'real' Australian literature. It avoids the easy translations of the visual arts, where paintings can be interpreted in New York as 'some kind of primitive abstraction.' It takes seriously, by necessity, the task of the translator, at which point we must theorise a bit about what is going on, and for this I can draw on my own experience in Broome.

A few years ago, Paddy Roe sang some songs that were composed by a Ngumbal woman some years before, and then helped me render them in English. Paddy spoke a few traditional languages from around Broome, plus Broome English. I never got the impression, when he was talking about languages, that they were clearly delineated from one another. Rather they were "bordering" on one another all the time.[1] There was no-one doing that nation-building work of separating languages off from one another, standardising and unifying them. In theorising translation, Naoki Sakai rather cleverly shows that the unity of language is in fact a modelling, and an effort of the imagination. No one ever experiences a language in all its unity, but what we do experience all the time are acts of translation. So, as he says, "translation is anterior to the organic unity of language and [...] this unity is posited through the specific representation of translation" (71).

We conventionally represent translation as bridging two languages, as a "communication model of equivalence and exchange," but that is not what it is, it is a "form of political labour to create continuity at the elusive point of discontinuity in the social" (72). Paddy Roe was working on creating continuity within the political grouping of the people called *Goolarabooloo*. This is not a 'tribe', since it is composed of different land-holding groups speaking different languages. It is a kind of political confederacy unified by 'lines' of significant ceremonies and responsibility for sites going down the coast from One Arm Point to south of Broome. So, what happened when I sat with Paddy Roe and we began to translate into English? The political labour was now across another social discontinuity: an Aboriginal cultural corpus can now link to a putative Australian nation, and the songs could now impinge upon what we think is the representation of the national literature. There are a lot of steps on that journey! So far, it is largely only Indigenous writers working in English genres who have mounted that national stage.

The complex process of translation spelled out by this extraordinary book—from a spirit being to Dyuŋgayan to Paddy Roe and Butcher Joe, to Ray Keogh to Stuart Cooke; from Nyigina to Broome English to Australian English; from oral production supplemented with gestures and sand drawings via tape recorders and notebooks to alphabetic script printed on paper—reinforces the idea that translation is emphatically never about *reducing* the number of mediations, nor indeed facilitating the transfer of meaning.

Without Ray Keogh's work this book would not have been possible. *The Bulu Line* might have halted, and not been repatriated to the community as it has now been in this book form. I got to know Ray

1 Naoki Sakai, "How do we count a language? Translation and Discontinuity," *Translation Studies* 2.1 (2009). p. 83

well when we worked in Broome in the 80s when he was doing the ethnomusicological recording that became his thesis. Ray loved to sing himself, and had a big resonant voice that often exploded into laughter. When working with the old men he would laugh, too, as he tried to get his tongue around those palatal sounds: *ny* and *dy*. And as he was transcribing expertly and meticulously he would sing the songs with them too, continuing the life of this Bulu. Who could have guessed that it would then travel to the University of Sydney, where Ray would sing the songs to ethnomusicology students in his classes, for some short years before he was taken from us?

Consider this surprising idea from Andreas Lommel, remembering fieldwork in the Kimberley in 1938:

> They, of course, taught the corroboree to others still roaming in the bush. I even met some Worora men months later in Broome who taught the corroboree for a fee to others who did not understand their language—this did not matter.
>
> The poet made his songs in the language of his tribe, but, for rhythm and sentimental reasons he changed the language so that some of his songs could not be translated.[2]

The idea that clear understanding might 'not matter' and that obscurity might even be introduced, leaves us with what Cooke is calling the 'haze', the necessary obscurity in translation, and in poetry itself, which is a precondition for its vitality and sustainability. I am anxiously optimistic about the rich possibilities that this work offers. Anxious about the loss of the corpus of oral traditions and those still waiting for translators, but optimistic about their hidden powers searching for new forms and for the right occasions to erupt into the open again.

Stephen Muecke
Sydney, January 2014

---

2 Andreas Lommel and David Mowaljarlai. "Shamanism in North-West Australia," *Oceania* 64.4 (June 1994). p. 281

This introduction first provides basic information about the Bulu songpoems before extending into a more detailed explication of nurlu poetics. For readers interested primarily in a basic introduction, I suggest reading only the first three sections.

N.B. In most cases, words from languages other than English will be italicised the first time that each appears. From thereafter the word's italicisation will cease.

An Introduction to Dyuŋgayan's *Bulu Line*

What is *The Bulu Line*?

As we'll find a number of times throughout this introduction, there is both a simple and a complicated answer to the above question. Simply, a 'line' is a complete cycle of songpoems; *The Bulu Line* is a collection of 17 nurlu songs, and three dances, from the West Kimberley. The original owner of the line was George Dyuŋgayan (c. 1900-c.1995), a Nyigina lawman of Goolarabooloo.

Nurlu songpoetry is one of three key genres of song in the West Kimberley region. The foremost genre consists of the poetry that forms part of ritual and contains vital knowledge about history, philosophy, and social and ecological relationships. The song cycle that runs along the coast to the north of Broome, part of which constitutes the renowned Lurujarri Heritage Trail, is one example of such poetry. It comes from *Bugarrigarra*, or what is often translated as 'The Law' or 'The Dreaming', and its contents can often be closed to men, women or children, and invariably to the uninitiated. Poetry like this is sacred, and comes from the creation beings that sung the country into existence; it forms part of the great poetic heritage of this continent.

At the opposite end of the spectrum, a second major, and rapidly growing, genre consists of music like hip-hop and country & western. This genre is defined by the fact that its songs have been composed by artists who are still alive.

Like this second genre, nurlu are relatively 'young' songs. But they are distinguished from Western styles because they arrive in people's dreams (ie. they're not 'composed' in the conventional sense of the term). Unlike the first genre, however, they don't come from The Dreaming. Instead, their composition is attributed to various spirits, either *balangan* (spirits of the dead) or *rai*. Rai are child-like forms, believed to cause pregnancy. As we'll see in the *Bulu*, they can change shape at will – often from one kind of bird to another (they seem to have a penchant for snipes). Traditionally it is thought that when in a dream state, a person's spirit can leave his body and come into contact with balangan and rai in the spirit world. The spirit beings will perform songs and dances about events in their world, and, if he's good enough, the person's spirit may be able to bring the material back to his own world when he wakes up. That person then 'owns' the songs, dances and any associated costumes or totems from his dreams.[3] Stephen Muecke writes of how another noted Broome songman, Butcher Joe Nangan, used to get his own nurlu:

> He used to wake at about three in the morning and sing. Sing the lines over and over and over, until he remembered them, I guess. Paddy [Roe] had put us two fellas together in the same camp out at Coconut Wells, in those early days, and Butcher Joe would get me to smuggle in a couple of cans of VB. We would smoke rollies and sip our warm beers in the tropical night, having a laugh. Then, well before dawn, that singing would half wake me. This was what was called his *nurlu*, coming through from his Aunty's spirit.[4]

The other defining feature of nurlu is their instrumentation. The songs are accompanied by pairs of boomerangs struck together and by bodily percussion like clapping or striking the thighs with cupped hands. The dances may also feature elaborate head gear and totems, known as *waŋgararra*, which are worn or carried by the performers. Like the Western songs of the second genre, however, nurlu songpoems and dances can be performed by all members of the community; usually they serve as a form of entertainment prior to more serious ceremonies. Up until the 1960s, they were performed mainly for Aboriginal audiences, but towards the end of last century they were opened to tourists and visitors with increasing frequency.

The spirit of Dyuŋgayan's late father, Bulu, gave him the *Bulu* series.[5] (After Dyuŋgayan's, and then Paddy Roe's, passing, the ownership

---

3 Keogh, Ray, "*Nurlu* Songs from the West Kimberley: an introduction," *Australian Aboriginal Studies*.1 (1989). p. 3
4 Muecke, Stephen, *Butcher Joe*, dOCUMENTA (13) N°054 (Ostfilden: Hatje Cantz, 2011). p. 4. Known as *Marinydyirinydyi*, Butcher Joe's nurlu was comprised of over 50 songs and associated dances.
5 Keogh, Ray, "*Nurlu* Songs of the West Kimberleys," PhD Thesis, University of Sydney, 1990. p. 40

of the songs was passed on to Phillip Roe, a Goolarabooloo elder and Paddy Roe's grandson.) Bulu appeared as a balangan in a series of Dyuŋgayan's dreams in a manner not dissimilar to what Muecke described regarding Butcher Joe. Both parts of the *Bulu* take place in Nyigina and Warrwa country, which stretches from the east of Broome to the eastern limits of the Fitzroy River. The first half of *Bulu* describes the journey that Dyuŋgayan's spirit took with Bulu and a group of rai through traditional Nyigina and Warrwa lands.

The second half of *Bulu* doesn't describe a single journey in the same way. Instead, the verses talk of isolated events and natural phenomena. There are, however, various important links between both parts of *Bulu*. These include particular motifs (water, rain and rainbow snakes, for example), along with the general location of each verse, and a distinctive poetics of haziness or obscurity, which we will look at in some more detail later.

Who Was George Dyuŋgayan?

Apart from his early years, the details of Dyuŋgayan's life are patchy. Keogh provides some useful biographical information,[6] which I include below, but perhaps the best sources regarding his later years could be found in the oral histories in and around Broome, and in the private field journals of other researchers like Muecke.

At some point around the beginning of the twentieth century, George Dyunggan was born in *Bidan* country, between Manguel Creek and Dampier Downs. Bidan is traditional *Uba* Nyigina country, with red soil and beefwoods. Bulu had four wives, the fourth of which was Dyuŋgayan's mother.

Between 1905 and 1910, Bulu took his family west to a sheep camp at a European station on the southern edge of the Roebuck Plains. According to Roe, Bulu's job was to pump water for the station. Also known as *Dyarrmaŋgunan*, the camp was in traditional Yawuru territory. Around 1912, Dyuŋgayan's mother had another son to a European father. This was Paddy Roe, Dyuŋgayan's half-brother and 20th century Broome icon.

6 Ibid. pp. 38-9

Bulu's was one of many Aboriginal families to move to the Roebuck Plains in the early 1900s; the influx of various language groups into the area resulted in what is now the characteristic cultural diversity of the Broome region. This occurred as part of a much larger drift of Aboriginal people in the West Kimberley, from their traditional lands to sheep and cattle stations, missions and towns. Keogh suggests a number of possible reasons for the dramatic shift from traditional country to more sedentary existences in the European centres. It may be, he says, that Aboriginal people had grown accustomed to European products in their diets, and therefore wanted continued access to them. The more plausible explanation, however, is that European domestic animals competed for resources with the native species, which placed severe pressures on the basis of the traditional food economy. Keogh also acknowledges that Yawuru women from the Roebuck Plains were blackbirded to work in the pearling and prostitution industries in in Broome; the subsequent shortage of Yawuru women on the Plains brought more women, along with their relatives, from the east and the south.[7]

Bulu's spirit now resides at a waterhole called *Wanydyal* (to the east of the Roebuck Plains). An island in the middle of two claypans, Wanydyal is the source from which all the verses and dances of *Bulu* emanate. Bulu's is a potent spirit, and often in close proximity to rai. The following is an extract from Keogh's field journal:

> Paddy told me a story about the power of the old man's [Bulu's] spirit – at a place called *maladya*[8] – that is, the old man's home – there are trees there that are completely out of place – they are surrounded by Tea Trees [paperbarks]. He [Paddy] and his old woman were camped there one night by themselves... Paddy's old woman got frightened as she saw all these falling stars. "Oh, that's the old man." Paddy believes that they were *rai* and that they were trying to see who was there – they were not falling stars, but in fact the lights used by the *rai* to light up the ground. Beautiful! Later that night Paddy was fast asleep, but was woken up by his wife – she could hear a car engine. Paddy knew it was the old man again...[9]

---

7 Ibid. p. 39
8 See Verse 7: *maladya* is the place in which Wanydyal is located.
9 Keogh, "*Nurlu* Songs of the West Kimberleys." p. 40. Many parts of

Bulu's son was blessed with extraordinary gifts. A *maban* (a 'clever man' or shaman), Dyuŋgayan was not only able to produce songpoetry of incredible beauty and power, but he had the ability to see and control things that others couldn't. In *Reading the Country*, Roe tells a story that gives us some insight into Dyuŋgayan's broader responsibilities:[10]

Back when Roe was still living at Dyarrmaŋgunan with Dyuŋgayan and the rest of the family, a man and a woman arrived one day from Mt. Anderson. The woman rightly belonged to a maban from another community, but the man had stolen her away. In his anger, the maban sent a rainbow snake (*yungurrugu*) to drown everyone at the sheepcamp. The snake unleashed a torrential downpour. Everyone was sleeping in the woolshed, but soon it began to break apart in the deluge. Only a maban can properly see yungurrugu, but the people in the shed could tell that the furious downpour was a manifestation of its presence. So Dyuŋgayan, still sound asleep, was called upon to fight the angry rainbow snake. By the time he'd woken up and realised what was happening, however, another snake from the sheepcamp's own waterhole had emerged to fight the intruder. After a savage battle, the camp snake defeated the maban's snake and chased it away, but in the aftermath it remained agitated and restless from the heat of the battle. It was Dyuŋgayan who had to calm the snake down so that it would return to its waterhole nearby.

When Keogh met Dyuŋgayan in the 1980s, he was living up at Coconut Wells (a little to the north of Broome) with Butcher Joe and Paddy Roe.

A Sum of Disparate Parts

According to Roe, Dyuŋgayan had only received Verses 1-8 of the *Bulu* before Roe left the sheep camp in 1929. After 1929, while still living at Dyarrmaŋgunan, Dyuŋgayan received other songs and dances

---

Keogh's journal contain restricted material, but the portion included here was included in his dissertation and is open to the public.

10 See Benterrak, Kim, Muecke, Stephen and Roe, Paddy, *Reading the Country: introduction to nomadology* (Fremantle: Fremantle Arts Centre Press, 1984). pp. 47-52

from Bulu. Roe and Dyuŋgayan referred to these songs as 'another line', even though they were still part of the *Bulu* corpus. *Bulu* was recorded and transcribed by musicologist Ray Keogh in the 1980s, with the help of Paddy Roe, Butcher Joe Nangan and Dyuŋgayan himself. The entire cycle was to become the basis of Keogh's doctoral research at the University of Sydney. In addition to transcriptions and glosses of the song verses themselves, Keogh also included extensive transcriptions of recorded conversations about the poetry in an appendix. These took place between Dyuŋgayan, Butcher Joe, Roe and himself, and were written and arranged according to many of the typographical innovations pioneered by Stephen Muecke in *Gularabulu* (1983).

Thus, the following pages contain the work of a group of Aboriginal and non-Aboriginal people, each of whom can claim limited amounts of authority regarding the result. While the English interpretations attached to the end of each 'Verse' are my own, the rest of the text has been transcribed and re-arranged, with minor edits, directly from Ray Keogh's Doctoral thesis, '*Nurlu* Songs of the West Kimberleys'. I have treated Keogh's thesis as a large body of found material, which I have cut up and reshaped to form the series of extended verses-in-translation that you see in this book. Consequently, the text you see collated together into one 'Verse' will often have origins in quite disparate parts of Keogh's thesis. For example, Verse 1 contains text from pages 92 & 93 – the main body of the dissertation – that has been interwoven with related material from Appendix 1 on page 277.

Of Keogh's transcriptions of conversations, many have been reproduced here. I have, however, made some slight changes in order to better-translate the oral origins of these texts. For example, orthographic features (such as commas, italics for non-English words, full stops and capitalisations) have been removed. Accordingly, syntactical pauses are indicated by larger-than-normal spaces between words. The line divisions are identical to those used by Keogh, however, and were determined by the speaker's falling intonation pattern (more on that later). In Keogh's glosses (which follow the Nyigina verses), 'ø' refers to a word without meaning (common in many Aboriginal song languages), or a word which Keogh did not understand, or which the others didn't translate for him. These 'silences' are reproduced in my own translations and are indicated by the bracketed blank spaces. They remind us that translation, in the words of Pierre Joris,

> has to be as literal as possible, that is to say, it has to adhere to the same absence/presence structure the poem uses… A translation should not, cannot make clearer what the original poem has purposefully hidden.[11]

The Songpoem as a Verse-in-Translation

The 'translation' of each verse that you're about to read is an extended and visually complex piece with multiple modes and a number of voices.[12] Each verse as a whole should be considered in the prism of the progressive present tense – as a 'verse-in-translation', rather than as a finalised 'translation' – because your reading will literally *generate* the translation. Without this movement of your eye across the space of the page, without the cognitive additions of the various kinds of data that you encounter as you read, none of it will make sense: read as isolated parts, the transcription of the verse in Nyigina at the start will be as opaque as my interpretation at the end.

Featured first and foremost at the beginning of each verse is its transcription in the original Nyigina, each of which is taken directly from Keogh's thesis. You'll notice that the number of lines varies from verse to verse: each verse of *Bulu* can be divided into these 'textual lines' because the beginning of each line corresponds to a descent in the tonic of the melody. Coming directly underneath the transcription, a gloss gives basic definitions for the songpoem's phrasal units. Then, depending on the conversations that Keogh had with the others, you'll see a number of mediations of the poem *through* the voices of Butcher Joe, Roe and/or Dyuŋgayan. My insertion of these mediating discussions 'into' the text of the songpoem is by no means an indulgent theoretical or aesthetic exercise, but rather is reflective of a situation common to much songpoetry translation. In a beautiful book

---

11 Joris, Pierre, *Justifying the Margins* (Cambridge: Salt, 2009). p. 23
12 For the theoretical background to this approach, see Cooke, Stuart, *Speaking the Earth's Languages: a theory for Australian-Chilean postcolonial poetics* (Amsterdam & New York: Rodopi, 2013). pp. 115-153

on the songlines of Carpentaria, John Bradley makes the comment that some of the Yanyuwa people he was working with were doubtful about the effectiveness of taping songpoetry, primarily because "the taped version doesn't allow the discussions that take place during the singing". "I understood all of this," Bradley continues, "and... felt the sterility of the process..."[13] Ronald Berndt, in the introduction to his now-classic *Love Songs of Arnhem Land*, is careful to emphasise that such discussions are absolutely integral to the translation process:

> Several men always joined in these discussions, so that no one song and its meaning or meanings depended on the singer alone, however knowledgeable he was considered to be. Then, and only then, was it possible to go on to the next song, when the process was repeated... it was the only way to check and re-check the songs and to obtain a deeper understanding...[14]

Indeed, Berndt noted that explanations were almost as integral to one of the song cycles as the performance of the cycle itself:

> One of the most interesting points about these songs is that explanations are always given. It was obvious that Aborigines themselves felt impelled to comment on each in order to make clear what they understood the words to mean...[15]

Nevertheless, Berndt is something of an omniscient narrator in *Love Songs*, providing long, scholarly explanations of each poem, and presenting the translations themselves as all but entirely separated from Aboriginal authority and repackaged as [stunningly beautiful] Western art objects. As Author and Translator, he retains the ultimate authority to open or close pathways of interpretation. A key difference in *The Bulu Line* is that Keogh's academic, whitefella summation, while positioned

---

13 Bradley, John (with Yanyuwa families), *Singing Saltwater Country: journey to the songlines of Carpentaria* (Sydney: Allen & Unwin, 2010). p. 214
14 Berndt, Ronald M., *Love Songs of Arnhem Land* (West Melbourne: Thomas Nelson, 1976). p. 45
15 Ibid. p. 138

in his own dissertation as a similarly [but more modestly] mediating voice of reason, is now part of the textual system. 'Flatter' than that of the others, Keogh's is a prosaic voice born of his scholarly training. Invariably, any conclusion or final statement he might like to make about the 'correct' version of a songpoem is rendered impossible: even after speaking to all the commentators, Keogh seems no closer to a 'true' reading than the others. This is sometimes made startlingly evident by Kim Ackerman's comments. After reviewing an earlier version of this manuscript, Ackerman, a pioneering anthropologist in the West Kimberley, found a number of problems with Keogh's analyses. I have noted his concerns where relevant.

And, while I'm positioning myself here in this introduction as something of a self-appointed expert on the material, you'll see that my own additions to each verse (those sections entitled 'Cooke') are anything but authoritative. It's important to emphasise that these are not my *translations* – the translation is a process composed of the entire text under the heading of each verse. Rather, the 'Cooke' additions are *interpretations*, or continuations of one or two possible trajectories that I've traced from Keogh's first gloss of the song text. Once you've read through the whole line a couple of times you might like to attempt your own. You could write them in under each of mine, and let the force of the *Bulu* keep rolling.

In this respect, these verses-in-translation are examples of the limited authority granted any one person in West Kimberley societies. Knowledge is invariably deferred: to the old if you're young, to the more initiated, or to the people in the next community in the story or songline in question. Roe would often say to Muecke, "That's all I can give you about that story, if you want the rest you had better go see so-and-so".[16] In these verses, limited authority is evident not only in the ways in which each speaker contributes small readings, but also in the way the *reader's* position is not allowed to rest comfortably with any one of the speaker's.

Nevertheless, some explanation of my 'interpretation' process is required. I didn't just translate a vague 'vibe'; I was keenly interested in the question of how to interpret each songpoem typographically,

---

16 Muecke, Stephen and Roe, Paddy, "Words from the Other Side," *Social Alternatives* 9.4 (1991). p. 27

and how to best translate its aesthetic features. These features include:

* *multiple beginnings:* The performance of a songpoem may begin at the start of any line in the song text; in the *Bulu*, as in many other genres of songpoetry, no one text line represents the 'beginning' of the songpoem. This is reflected in my own interpretations by the rotation of the first line in each successive stanza – that is, if there are 3 textual lines in a verse, then I will have composed 3 stanzas to show the three possible permutations: '1, 2, 3', then '2, 3, 1' and '3, 1, 2'. If there are only two textual lines, then two stanzas will show the permutations '1, 2' and '2, 1'. It's like one of Jason Nelson's marvellous online 'poetry cubes', where you turn the poem around with your mouse to look at its different surfaces.

* *the text loop:* In performance, the text can be repeated several times until the melody has been completed. This produces a loop, where the 'end' of the text joins up with the 'beginning' again, and the cycle continues until the end of the song. I've translated this by making the last line of my versions very similar to the first, and by leaving them open-ended with ellipses to suggest that they aren't yet concluded, but could keep looping if required. Importantly, the last line of my interpretation is never *identical* to the first because the aesthetic characteristics of the text line always depend upon its relationship to the rhythmic structure (sometimes syllables have to be discarded in order to better 'match' the rhythmic requirements) and to its position in the melody (whether it is being sung at the start, middle or end of the descent – see below). However, it is not the case that the precise wording of individual text lines always changes so drastically within a single performance – indeed, the wording might not change at all. Rather, I'm trying to convey the *overall* flexibility of the line as a musical *and* poetic artefact.

* *the descending melody:* Melody in *Bulu* is composed of several cyclical repetitions of a descent over the range of a ninth or tenth, and each descent has a structure typical of many Central Australian melodies.[17] In performance, the melody descends in tonic at the beginning of each textual line; each live performance will comprise of one or two major

17 Keogh, "*Nurlu* Songs of the West Kimberleys." p. 211

vocal descents.[18] That aural situation has become a visual one here: like a descending tonic, a shrinking font produces a steady change in the relationship between the poetic language and the surrounding space. My interpretations are not intended to be accurate translations of the musical performance, however, so each change in the font size is not meant to suggest that the melody would descend at the same points, or with identical frequency, in a live performance. As with other aspects of my interpretative process, I have been more interested in honouring the aesthetic energy of the *Bulu* than in producing a scholarly, musicological document.

the absence of a dominant subjectivity: The reader will also note the obfuscation of actors in most of the verses: in the Nyigina, subjects will be occasionally identified in the third person, but where the prefix refers to the first person the identity is pluralised, or never stated at all.[19] This suggests indifference both to the distinction between the singular and plural subjects, and to a clear distinction between the singer and the other actors in his poetry. Apart from a couple of exceptions in the latter verses, pronouns are always in first- or third-person plural in my interpretations

the affective charge of the poetry: The *Bulu* is a communal poetics on all kinds of different levels: it draws Dyuŋgayan into relations with Bulu's spirit, with rai and with country; it draws people together to perform and to watch its performance; it attracts whitefellas from all over the country to learn about it and write about it and translate it; it's the responsibility not only of Dyuŋgayan but of a number of men across a number of generations. Bulu's spirit is an enormously potent charge that draws spaces and times into proximity, therefore. My final addendums to each songpoem are the consequences of this charge after it has travelled through Dyuŋgayan, Roe, Butcher Joe and Keogh, and then through me – my interpretations are tributes to the spirit of Bulu. Once I'd realised that the spirit of the poetry emerged as much from the song text as from between its fissures (as gloss and discussion), once the passage *between* my readings of these texts had

18 Ibid., p. 9
19 Ibid., pp. 77-8

acquired as much importance as the reading of each section itself, then it was my task to continue the passage, to prevent its conclusion. Call it an ethical responsibility, if you will – to care for life, be it corporeal or otherwise.

We need to be wary of judging translations of songpoetry solely on their capacity to reveal the aesthetic beauty of the poem in its original language. In his extraordinary *Songs of Central Australia*, T. G. H. Strehlow wrote of Aranda songpoetry that it was extremely ornamental, efficacious, thrilling and beautiful. Yet this ornamentation made translation a very difficult task, he said: despite his remarkable bilingual abilities, Strehlow lamented losing the poetry's ever-changing rhythms, the word-weaving into new and stimulating patterns, the venerability of its archaic diction, and the words rich in legendary associations. The best couplets, he said, had such an excellent style and diction that they were virtually untranslatable.[20]

There is no doubt – and, indeed, it could be a truism – to say that the songpoem undergoes irreversible changes upon its translation into English script. But what we don't learn from Strehlow's account is how this 'loss' of beauty can have a particular protective (and therefore *positive*) function. For in a work like *Songs of Central Australia* the reader's experience of the songpoem is not of the translation on its own, as if it were lost in space; rather, the experience is one of the translation *coupled with* Strehlow's explanation of how, in a previous language, this poem was exponentially more impressive.

In such instances the contextualisation of the poetry means that we as readers are aware of its beauty, but we can only imagine it. That which is sacred has not been described, catalogued or reduced but its importance hasn't been forgotten, either. So, when a scholar like David Abram writes of how, on the "flat and featureless terrain of the page" many Aboriginal songs and stories "begin to lose their Dreaming power" because they have been removed from the landscape to which they are connected, what's neglected is the possibility that this 'loss' could be a productive aspect of the translation.[21] As Jerome Rothenberg writes,

---

20 Strehlow, T. G. H., *Songs of Central Australia* (Sydney: Angus & Robertson, 1971). p. 246
21 Abram, David, *The Spell of the Sensuous: perception and language in a more-than-*

the ethical imperative of the translation of such work is

> not simply to make clear the world of the original, but
> to do so at some remove from the world itself: to reflect
> the song without the 'danger' of presenting any part of it
> (the melody, say) exactly as given: thus to have it while not
> having it, in deference to the sense of secrecy & localization
> that's so important to those for whom the songs are sacred
> & alive. So the changes resulting from translations are, in
> this instance, not only inevitable but desired...[22]

What conventional criticism wants to do when reading poetry is
something akin to restoring causality after the fact. The Conventional
Critic wants to know *why* the poet wrote it that way, and s/he's
uncomfortable if s/he doesn't see *how* the way the poem's composed
correlates nicely with what the poet wanted it to be *about*. In
Conventional Criticism, the poem doesn't have a life (and an agency)
of its own, but rather it represents life, which occurs somewhere
'outside' of the poem. Conventional Criticism relies on a distinction
that takes us all the way back to the dawn of the West:

> ...'poetry', since Aristotle, and since Plato, has been
> founded on... a distinction: *mimesis*. Its assumption: the
> administrable de*limitation* of the mimed (or mimable) and
> the mime, the presentation and the representation, the
> original (the thing referred to or imagined, the verisimilar
> signified) and the copy (the work or poem, creation or
> operation, the significant redundancy of noise).[23]

By the rationale of Aristotelian mimesis, if you translate a poem then
you can only ever step further away from the authentic "presentation"
that it is purported to represent. Translation always 'fails to capture'
whatever it was that the first language tried but, ultimately, also

---

human world, 1997 ed. (New York: Vintage, 1996). p. 177

22   Rothenberg, Jerome, *Pre-Faces & Other Writings* (New York: New
Directions, 1981). p. 85

23 Ajens, Andrés, *Poetry after the Invention of América: don't light the flower*,
trans. Michelle Gil-Montero (New York: Palgrave Macmillan, 2011). p. 95

failed to 'capture' itself. By the very same rationale, in the case of Aboriginal songpoetry the Conventional Critic can lay a charge against the translator for a) not properly 'revealing' the conditions for the composition of the poem, and therefore not properly 'revealing' the poem's meaning, or b) not properly acknowledging that said conditions can't be understood properly (because songpoetry is necessarily *other* and we cannot know what we know about it already – our knowledge is just redundant "noise").

Such Conventional Criticism – however commonplace – strikes me as absurd. On one level, it would seem to be a miracle that Aboriginal and non-Aboriginal people could communicate *at all*, not to mention the long and rich dialogues between Aboriginal and Settler cultures in all kinds of fields (here, Papunya art – thanks to Geoffrey Bardon – isn't as 'authentic' as the unreproducible traditional practices it sources!). Conventional Criticism ignores the fact of language as innumerable processes of *production*, as systems of meaning- and texture-making. We don't admonish the leaf for failing to look like the trunk of its tree. We don't say, upon the birth of a new child, 'What a shame that it only partially resembles the mother!' Rather, the translation is a *production* of the poem, a result of the neuro-chemical excitement it engendered in the head of the translator, a sign of its irrepressible energy. Indeed, the *poetry* itself isn't really in one language or another, but it occurs somewhere before and after it: something demands of the writer that it be written; alternatively, something occurs – not on the page but somewhere around it – to the reader when the poem is read. Lots of Aboriginal people might say that the 'something' demanding that the poem be written is country – or, more specifically, certain spirits who reside within country.

This alternative understanding of 'poetry', where the poem takes us forward into a new event, where we don't dig in and insist on finding discrete objects and emotions buried under each of the words, is vital to the way we approach and understand the following series of translations. The 'original beauty' of the *Bulu* hasn't been 'lost' or reduced in some proportional way. Rather, it's all still there, spread across country, across the pages and pages of Keogh's notes, and flashing across the pages of this book.

The Event(s) of Our Reading(s)

I must emphasise above all else that these are translations of the *event* of each songpoem (where an 'event' is, in the words of Gilles Deleuze, "a splitting off from, a breaking with causality; it is a bifurcation, a lawless deviation, an unstable condition that opens up a new field of the possible."[24]). Each verse-in-translation is indicative of the dynamic, communal and open-ended nature of nurlu songpoetry and poetics. Many other translations have treated Aboriginal songpoems as if they had always been written down by one author as one structure with one intention. Such assumptions are grossly reductive because they ignore a fundamental feature of much Aboriginal poetics: there is no single authority, nor a 'correct' poem waiting to be translated, but rather a matrix of country, text and rhythm that can manifest in a variety of forms, depending on the context. For these reasons as much as any other, the following translations are manifest as numerous registers, voices and styles.

In the *Bulu*, what was a live performance of music, dance and poetry has been translated to a no-less live performance of language, typography and poetry. Your reading of it – your selection of which path to follow, and how, and with what knowledge – is another kind of performance, another kind of event, producing an uncertainty and unrepeatability akin to the structure of the original song text. Dyuŋgayan's songpoems describe events, and their performances translate the events into a communal space. Now the translation has continued yet further, and into different spaces.

The single biggest problem with many previously published translations of Aboriginal songpoetry is that they neglect the *processes* by which the translations came to be. The poets themselves, who invariably spend many hours at the side of the linguist or musicologist to assist with their translations, are almost completely removed from the texts that result. The poetry is treated as a product, rather than a communal event. In *The Bulu Line* I have begun with a different premise: a primary requirement for songpoetry translation is that the textual transcriptions are not interpreted as static representations of

24 Deleuze, Gilles, *Two Regimes of Madness*, trans. A. Hodges and M. Taormina (New York: Semiotext(e), 2006). p. 215

an ideal performance in a distant time and place, but as performances in themselves. From this perspective, each translation of a songpoem is an irresolvable nexus of Aboriginal and colonial knowledges.

Next to the notion of the Poem as something written next to the left-margin of a page, the sheer aesthetic range of songpoetry is quite astonishing. Rothenberg writes of songpoetry that:

> [it] was almost always part of a larger situation (ie. was truly intermedia), [so] there was no more reason to present the words alone as independent structures than the ritual-events, say, or the pictographs arising from the same source. Where possible, in fact, one might present or translate all elements connected with the total 'poem'...[25]

We could say that, as songpoems involve multiple media in performance, the verses-in-translation gathered here involve multiple registers of writing. But this is wouldn't be a satisfactory response to the quote. Although the above passage is decades old, Rothenberg's work remains pertinent because it alerts us to the multiple levels on which a songpoem functions and, like a script or a libretto, the way that the poetry runs like a spine through all of these elements. Because, even if the songpoem performance is recorded as film or produced as digital animation, any subsequent engagement with it will always begin with a question about what is *happening*, and this question will always require another question about how to best guide the song language into the English language (so that we might find a kind of *answer*). The songpoem's journey into writing needs as its destination the most accommodating, unsettling and evocative kind of discourse we can summon. This, of course, is the discourse of poetry.

---

25 Rothenberg, *Pre-Faces & Other Writings*. p. 96. Rothenberg refers to songpoetry as 'tribal poetry'.

Bulu Haze

One of the aspects of the *Bulu* that intrigues me most is the centrality of what we might call a poetics of uncertainty. Here, meaning – and, more than meaning, the very *clarity* we might require to ascertain it – is a wobbly, ephemeral concept, akin perhaps to the Kimberley horizon in the middle of the day. Keogh takes great pains to point out that the difficulties of determining a clear understanding of the songpoetry don't arise so much from some kind of inability – whether on the part of the whitefella observer (Keogh and/or me), the authorities like Paddy Roe or Butcher Joe, or Dyuŋgayan himself – to discover a fixed interpretation, as they do from "an intrinsically fluid relationship" between the various components of each poem.[26] This situation stems from a number of sources, the precise importance of each with relation to the *Bulu* is indeterminate. On the one hand, as I mentioned before it is common for West Kimberley songpoetry to have various levels of meaning, depending on one's level of initiation or familiarity with the material. On the other hand, texts can be interpreted in multiple ways because the song text is quite different to spoken language, most particularly in the sense that it isn't separated into discrete words but is actually 'agglutinated' combinations of different words and non-semantic syllables. It's also entirely possible that different internal rhythmic constructions may be associated with different levels of meaning, regardless of the content of the text.[27]

A useful example is the penultimate verse in *The Bulu Line*. According to Paddy Roe, Verse 16 is about Bulu's rai giving sanction for all the songpoems, dances and paraphernalia associated with *Bulu* to be made public. For Dyuŋgayan and Butcher Joe, however, Verse 16 tells of how Bulu's spirit now dwells in a *dyila* (waterhole), thus associating him with rainmaking activity. This, they say, reflects the close relationship of the song with Bugarrigarra and with country. That there are two interpretations of a songpoem amongst three such knowledgeable commentators is no accident, either. Multiple interpretations of the *Bulu* are basically endemic to the material. Of the eleven songpoems discussed by more than one individual with Keogh, nearly half were

---

26 Keogh, "*Nurlu* Songs of the West Kimberleys." pp. 78-9
27 Ibid. p. 81

interpreted quite differently by different commentators.[28]

Verse 9 is a particularly interesting example in this regard. For Paddy Roe, this verse isn't part of the eight verses of the first half of *Bulu*. Instead, the verse commemorates the appearance of a comet passing over their sheep camp, Dyarrmaŋguyan, after the journey of the first 8 verses had long been completed. Dyuŋgayan, on the other hand, would sing Verse 9 (and also 10) *before* Verse 6 as a part of the primary *Bulu* journey. Doing so arranges the poems in a chronological order, where the 'star' in Verse 9 is a morning star, and the sign for the ensuing sunrise, which is the subject of Verse 6. By incorporating Verse 9 into the previous series of eight songpoems, Dyuŋgayan 'de-contextualised' Verse 9 and expanded the range of the first eight verses, thereby showing how adaptable his *Bulu* could be.

Verse 3 produces an intriguing disagreement, where Keogh is left none the wiser as to whose interpretation might be [the most] correct. The disjuncture occurs around the differing interpretations of a single word. Butcher Joe thinks the word is *galdyiri* ('tree snake'), because for him the poem relates to watersnake mythology. Roe, on the other hand, is convinced that the word is *galydyi* ('white ochre'). For Roe, Verse 3 is about getting white ochre for use during ceremony. Somewhat frustratingly for Keogh, it turns out that Dyuŋgayan agrees with *both* Butcher Joe and Roe! As I note in a footnote to Verse 3, in light of the discrepancy between snake and white ochre, it's interesting to consider that snake faeces are generally white…

At any rate, in the cases of Verses 3 and of 16, it might not be that a commentator is 'wrong' – it might not be, in other words, that a commentator can't remember the 'true' meaning of the poem. What we see happening, rather, is the gradual replacement of 'historical' references with 'mythological' ones. In the process of Verse 3, Dyuŋgayan is literally catalysing this change by allowing for both Roe's factual and Butcher Joe's mythological interpretations. As the origins of the song recede further into the past, the poetry, like all history, sheds its chronological exactitude to become subsumed in the timeless (or, more accurately, time-*full*) presence of The Dreaming. Time and space transform the songpoetry from the work of balangan to the work of

---

28 Ibid. p. 85-6

'the creative period' of Bugarrigarra.[29]

But more interesting still, I think, is how the uncertainty is present at the lexical level of the song text, in subsequent discussions about translation *and* in the content of the *Bulu* itself. Much of the journey in the first half of *Bulu* is marked with interruptions, uncertainties, and vectorial changes. In Verse 6, for example, the group sees a mountain or a ridge in the distance. Roe believes this verse tells of the group's journey north-west from Balgandyirr towards Malarra (Mt. Clarkson). Unlike so many instances in Western lyric poetry, where a poem's value is determined by its ability to bring images into sharp relief – the poem's capacity to produce clarity, in other words – here the group can't actually see the mountain very clearly because they are still a long way away: *marrarri*, says Roe, means "can't see properly". Crucially, this lack of visual precision implies the absence of any immediately obvious landmark or physical referent, so it seems to necessitate a different reading. Dyuŋgayan, then, says that the verse actually refers to Garrawin, a ridge to the *west* of Mt. Clarkson. Malarra, he says, is not Mt. Clarkson. Furthermore, instead of 'marrarri', Dyuŋgayan sang the verse with the phrase *barrarri*, which refers to 'sun' or 'sunrise'. This was the verse he would always perform after verses 9 and 10 (discussed above) in order to further develop the motif of the dawn.

From a poetics of uncertainty, we might [try to] zoom in on an associated poetics of *haziness* or *obscurity*. As Verse 6 suggests, sight by no means reigns supreme in a large number of *Bulu* verses. As lines of the poetry might flicker with morphing words, so does watersnake into white ochre, or Mt. Clarkson into Garrawin. Often, the sheer size of the space around the group means that things in the distance are difficult to discern: in Verse 6 it's the shape of a mountain, but in Verse 2 they seem to see a flock of birds. The eyes are of little more use in the second half of *Bulu*, either. Verse 12 describes a group of rai in the darkness, but Dyuŋgayan can barely make them out. (How many Western poems centre on figures that the poet can't really see?) Indeed, even in Verse 13, when the rai come in to full view to start dancing, there's still uncertainty between the interpreters as to whether or not it *was* a group of rai, or actually Bulu himself. "The dancer was Bulu," writes Keogh, "but when they looked closer he had gone." The

---

29 Ibid. pp. 88-9

remaining verses continue to delve into a world of alternating forms that shimmer on the cusp of their realisation.

In nurlu poetry, crystalline descriptions of scenes aren't as important as are the ways that these scenes can fit within larger narratives. Images aren't assembled as disjunctive collages, in other words, but are part of a dynamic environment of multiple meanings. We'll soon see that the coherence of a line of verse within a rhythmic structure is also more important than the exact replication of that line in each reiteration.

'Songpoetry'… 'song'… 'poetry'… 'literature'…?

You might be wondering by this point: What of my glossing over the differences between music and literature? How can I so easily equate 'song' with 'poetry'? Aren't I ignoring all kinds of crucial distinctions when I bring each word together to insist on the 'songpoem'? What sort of gross, colonialist move is going on here?

To respond to these questions, let us call to attention the Western origins of the various categories that I've just listed. To paraphrase what Chilean poet and critic Andrés Ajens argues regarding American (ie. North *and* South) poetry, in order to speak of an indigenous art like 'songpoetry', "we must be aware that this speaking cannot occur in the domain of literature, for literature is something already situated, thought out, in, and from the terrain of Western Europe."[30] "Literature is a Western *matter*," he says, in both conceptual and material terms.[31] But this doesn't preclude the possibility of something else, what Ajens calls "a category of openly intermixed-up writing", or writing that operates with an indigenous/Western 'double register', as well as

> the dual or multiple referentiality of traditions themselves (and perhaps the suspension of all traditional belonging) to create their (not) own, im/proper condition of im/possibility.[32]

---

30 Moure & Gander in Ajens, *Poetry after the Invention of América.* p. xii
31 Ibid. p. 85
32 Ibid. p. 87

In terms that are perhaps more familiar, my goal here is not to incorporate 'songpoetry' within a Western body of 'poetry', not to claim ownership of West Kimberley poetics within a broader field of 'our' poetics, not to provide thrilling "disruptions or disjunctive possibilities" for reinvigorating our own sense of the poem.[33] Rather, the aim is very much to grant songpoetry its unsettled position as both-poem-and-song *and* not-poem-or-song. I'm not interested in denying the possibilities for translations between traditions – an absurd and necessarily insatiable desire if ever there was one! – but instead I want to emphasise "a certain dwelling and even lingering in translation",[34] to paraphrase Ajens again, who also asks:

> What about writing that refuses to erase or even recombine the differences between traditions of inscription, but rather, by bringing them face to face and exposing them, makes way for an encounter between different cultural provenances and languages?[35]

To change direction a little, I'll also answer the questions I put forward above in another way (as I said at the start, many questions will have several answers). Let's assume for the moment that our categories of 'song', 'music' and 'poetry' are broad enough to decentre any Eurocentric notions of them. Let's then assume that with our broader, more flexible understanding of what might constitute 'poetry' that we could propose to make a distinction between Aboriginal *song* (which might have elements of poetry) and Aboriginal song*poetry*. To understand the compelling structural distinctions between 'songs' and West Kimberley songpoetry, we are best served by returning to Strehlow, who remains perhaps our only scholar equally qualified in both Aboriginal and Western literary traditions.

Like nurlu in the West Kimberley, throughout Central and Western Australia there are whole corpuses of songpoetry and accompanying dances that have originated quite recently (within the past 100 years) from various spirit beings in country. We're able to use Strehlow's *Songs*

---

33 See Moure & Gander in ibid. p. xiv
34 Ibid. p. 157
35 Ibid. p. 6

of Central Australia in a discussion of *Bulu* nurlu because, according to Keogh, nurlu songpoetry shares relations not only with songpoetry from other parts of the Kimberley, but also with Western and Central Australian genres. These related genres include the *purlapa* of the Walpiri, the *turlku* of the Pintupi and the *ltarta* of the Alyawarra and Aranda peoples.[36] Specifically, both the nurlu and Central and Western Desert songpoetry consist of a short text which is repeated several times in the performance (this is often referred to as a 'word group' in the scholarly literature). Then, a repeating rhythmic unit or 'rhythmic pattern' of the same length as the word group has a fixed relation to the word group. A rhythmic accompaniment, which maintains a fixed relationship to the word group and the rhythmic pattern, produces the 'rhythmic text'. Thirdly, placed 'on top' of this inextricable text-rhythm molecule is a "flexible melodic contour", which can move quite independently of the rhythmic text.[37] The *textual-rhythm*, therefore, and not the melodic character of a regular song, is very much the basis of the nurlu songpoem.

The Aranda songpoetry that Strehlow discusses in *Songs of Central Australia* shares many of the qualities of early European church chants, most of which are intoned, chanted or sung with simple instruments to emphasise the beats. All such chants are clearly marked from prose forms by their rhythmic measure and rather peculiar sentence construction.[38] However, Strehlow also emphasises that Central Australian song*poems* are *not* exact equivalents of modern Western *songs*. In Western song, musical values are all-important: each song has its own rhythm and melodic outline, which is divided into bars with notes of a definite and regular time. There is an insistence on the harmony, melody and rhythm of musical sounds, rather than on the melody, formal shape or rhythm of the accompanying words. According to Strehlow, the best Western songs are generally lyrics which are simple enough to be improved by music, whereas the more complex lyrics – those which are more poetic – are often marred with music because their different rhythms conflict.[39]

On the other hand, the two principal rules in Central Australian

---

36 Keogh, "*Nurlu* songs from the West Kimberley." pp. 3-4
37 Ibid. p. 6
38 Strehlow, *Songs of Central Australia*. p. 4
39 Ibid. pp. 9-10

songpoetry are, firstly, that the singer adhere to the traditional rhythmic pattern proper to the songpoem and, secondly, that the singer begin the songpoem on the highest note, and end on the lowest. The songpoems are not 'sung' in the Western sense and, because of their lyrical complexities, Strehlow argues that it would be unfair to judge them with purely musical criteria. After all, the majority of a line's syllables are intoned in the same note. But furthermore, like church chants, songpoems are largely built on verses composed as couplets, and each couplet is a structurally discrete rhythmic and semantic unit.[40]

However, the association of songpoetry with church chant is complicated by certain endemic features of the former. In Central Australian songpoetry, the strong beat of a clear rhythmic measure takes prominence, moulding words into new forms, and reshaping the language of speech into the language of poetry. It is the rhythmic measure that *produces* the poetry: it changes the speech accent and the phonetic qualities of the words; syllables are frequently inserted into words in order to 'stretch' the prose to fit into the rhythmic unit; the rhythmic text can often completely obliterate the divisions between words in a line.[41] In the case of the *Bulu*, Keogh finds a relatively high proportion of lexical items from everyday Nyigina: about 80% of the song words are also in regular language. Nevertheless, all of the words are subject to modification. Words might be lengthened by adding affixes with no semantic value, by duplicating part of a word (*dyularra* might become *dyularralarra*, for example), or by modifying and duplicating the end of a word (*rjanbala* might become *rjanbalinbali*). Words might also undergo phonetic changes: *malady* could become *malanydyi; milydyidawurru* could become *milydyidawurruy*.[42]

In European chants, however, words undergo no such transformations. The varying lengths of the couplets alter the musical pattern, corresponding with the modern European principle that a verse's rhythm must not destroy the normal accentuation (as in English) or spoken rhythm (as in French) that the words would bear in prose or speech. Composers treat the chant as a musical composition to which words have to be *fitted*. While the melodic structure remains

40 Ibid. p. 10
41 Ibid. p. 57, 64
42 Keogh, "*Nurlu* Songs of the West Kimberleys." pp. 65-6

intact, the rhythmic text is altered in order to preserve the regular spoken rhythm of the lyric. Central Australian Aboriginal practice is the direct opposite: the speech accents of language are refused by the strong rhythmic patterns of the verse.[43]

My earlier proposition, then, that the word (or, more strictly, the unit of language-rhythm) has a higher priority in West Kimberley songpoetry than in Western song, might now seem counter-intuitive: isn't the word accorded greater importance in Western song because the natural prose rhythm of speech is maintained in the music, so that musical patterns must bend around it? The answer to this objection is 'no', for two reasons. Firstly, West Kimberley and Central Australian songpoetry represents the valorisation of *poetic* language over the spoken language that it transforms. As I said earlier, the poetic – rather than the spoken – text (ie. the rhythmic text) becomes the defining unit of the song. 'Mixing' of a language into a 'new' form is not a corruption or denigration of the language but, quite to the contrary, the very condition necessary for it to be *alive*.[44]

Secondly, the objection doesn't account for the effect of the prioritisation of natural prose rhythms. To continue with the earlier comparison, in European chant music a series of devices can be formulated to allow the chant rhythm to give way to words without destroying the rhythmical unity of the harmonic structure.[45] This means that the harmonic structure – the foundation of the chant – remains intact despite any apparent allowances it makes to the words it incorporates. As the history of avant-garde poetics in the West has shown us, however, the creation of new languages and grammars can be as surprising and captivating as any melody. Western song lyrics are largely subservient to their melodies; indeed, in many songs their comprehension is almost irrelevant to our enjoyment of them (this also says something about the enormous popularity of English-language songs in many non-English speaking countries). In most English songs, text is an independent structure to the 'tune', where 'tune' has both rhythm and melody. Different verses or texts can be put to the same tune and the song can still be regarded as the same song. Where text

43 Strehlow, *Songs of Central Australia*. p. 11
44 See Ajens, *Poetry after the Invention of América*. p. 30
45 Strehlow, *Songs of Central Australia*. p. 11

is independent of melody and rhythm, texts become interchangeable and therefore inessential components of songs.

In contrast, rhythmic-text and melody are independent in songpoetry like nurlu. Here, the substitution of a different text while maintaining the same melody and rhythm would be regarded as either incorrect or a different song.[46] In songpoetry, in other words, the text has a primary visibility. Where melody is independent of text and rhythm, and text and rhythm are always interrelated in the form of a 'rhythmic text', text is a fundamental component of the song. As such, nurlu songpoems often set the same rhythmic text to different parts of the melody, so that it is the melody which becomes interchangeable. In Central Australian (and West Kimberley) songpoetry, the poetic rhythm doesn't flow directly from the rhythms of speech; it is, says Strehlow, incompatible with the inclinations of spoken language. Rather, poetic language brings with it particular rhythmic patterns that restructure syntactical relations. Songpoetry is "a mould," writes Strehlow, into which "everyday speech is melted and reshaped".[47]

This isn't to neglect the musical qualities of the songpoetry, either, which are impossible to ignore. While it is clear that many songpoems "have certain musical characteristics that correspond closely to what we call tunes", it remains the case that basic musical notation of the verses presents "very considerable difficulties". Primarily, this is because "there is no fixed, invariable melody in our sense of the word".[48] Indeed, looking at some of Keogh's transcripts provides perfect illustration of the situation: often the melodic contours are so subtle as to be almost imperceptible.[49] Accordingly, Strehlow stresses that in these songpoems, "music is still the servant of the words". The main functions of the music are to emphasise the stresses in the poetry, and to give a time value to the syllables of the rhythmic measures, which have reshaped the words of the couplets into forms that can be performed by a group of singers.[50]

---

46 Turpin, Myfany, "The Poetics of Central Australian Song," *Australian Aboriginal Studies*. 2 (2007). p. 101
47 Strehlow, *Songs of Central Australia*. p. 19
48 Ibid. p. 40
49 Eg. Verse 16 in Keogh, "*Nurlu* Songs of the West Kimberleys." pp. 257-8
50 Strehlow, *Songs of Central Australia*. p. 32

To return to the irresolvable multi-valency of the songpoem that I raised earlier, however, as much as we can prioritise its song text we are still unable to do away altogether with the fact the songpoem is thoroughly situated within the world of sound. Most English poems are written according to the rhythms of speech and are to be read aloud or recited. Central Australian and West Kimberley songpoems, by contrast, are based on *musical* rhythms. They can never be recited, but must be intoned or chanted according to traditional rhythmic measures and tonal patterns (which have to be learnt by heart for each verse).[51] Accordingly, the smallest unit of measure in a *Bulu* couplet isn't the 'foot' of English poetry but the *smallest rhythmic phrase*. In non-musicological terms, this means that a typographical arrangement of the poetry into 'couplets' that we can 'read', like the ones Strehlow includes in *Songs*, might look like songpoetry translated into English, but in reality the arrangement buries the musical structuring of the language beneath the conventions of English verse.

On the one hand this is a problem without solution because an oral poetics is always going to leave something behind when it ventures onto the page. But, as I discussed earlier, the crucial point is that the translation *acknowledges what has been translated*; this acknowledgement, in turn, has a productive value. Thus, my interpretations here are not politely requesting that we read them as lyrical poems. So, while they can of course be read without recourse to an explicitly musical structure, certain features nevertheless imbue the texts with a rhythmic quality unrelated to speech rhythms: the split lines enforce a rhythmic pause that's unrelated to orders of metric feet; the shrinking font provides a visual cue that structures the phrasing in a way that's unrelated to the semantic content. So the music has not been 'translated' in a literal sense, but a clear sign of the poetry's heritage in oral Aboriginal musical structure remains, and an unusual, visual poetry is the result.

A big part of the 'problem' comes, of course, from our understanding of 'translation'. Here I'll turn to Ajens again, who identifies two distinct but related senses of the term:

> First of all, translation as the transport of a signified at the
> price of sacrificing a signifier (transmigration of the soul

---

51 Ibid. p. 89

between bodies) or, similarly, the transport of an ideality of sense between unequal containers (practically the entire history of translation in the West…). That is, translation in the regular or conventional sense of the term, Oedipal transference or transport included…[52]

It's our obsession in the West with translation as "the transport of an ideality of sense" that causes much whitefella discussion about songpoetry translation to run aground. There's something 'behind' the words that gets lost (but which must be conquered!), we object. Or, How can another form hold the contents of the first? Ajens hereby raises the possibility of a different sense of translation:

> an *entirely new* sense perhaps, a sense not entirely assured beforehand, a sense oscillating or still to come—and which, for that reason, might never come—rendering the metaphysics of the sign (the ease of separating signified and signifier) immediately ineffective and leaving (despite all possible effort to transport the ideality of the meaning or the matter) such transport open to accident…

Here, with the potential for "accident", Ajens sees the possibility for the "*transference* of an event" as "singular and unforeseeable" as any originary genesis.[53] Turning to Jaques Derrida, for whom translations are instances of "Oedipal transference", he proposes something else that, "while still going by the name translation", is not driven by the same need for semblance to its origin/al. This other kind of translation is instead driven by the event as it takes place – where the event represents what Derrida calls "a history of the unique".[54] This translation is a singular, irreversible instance, where the possibilities of the poem crystallise as this or that place in time, as this or that remarkably unpredictable constellation of experience. The event is the opening of a region in which the poem comes into contact with an economy; the event is the *anatomy* of the translation itself. The *Bulu's* irruption into time could only have been a pure surprise for

---

52 Ajens, *Poetry after the Invention of América.* pp.128-9
53 Ibid. p. 129
54 Ibid. p. 130

Dyuŋgayan. After all, who knows what'll happen when you fall asleep? In Dyuŋgayan's case, he found himself wandering through country with the spirit of his late father and a mob of rai. In a region so thoroughly unimagined or unexpected, the only way to recount it for everyone else on waking was to turn it into songpoetry. And of the songpoetry, of the event of each songpoem, well, the only way to continue this history of surprises was to create another, altogether different, set of poems in its wake.

Stuart Cooke
Gold Coast, 2014

Bibliography

Abram, D. *The Spell of the Sensuous: perception and language in a more-than-human world.* 1997 ed. New York: Vintage, 1996.

Ajens, A. *Poetry after the Invention of América: don't light the flower.* Trans. Gil-Montero, Michelle. New York: Palgrave Macmillan, 2011.

Benterrak, K., Muecke, S., and Roe, P. *Reading the Country: introduction to nomadology.* Fremantle: Fremantle Arts Centre Press, 1984.

Berndt, R. M. *Love Songs of Arnhem Land.* West Melbourne: Thomas Nelson, 1976.

Bradley, J. (with Yanyuwa Families). *Singing Saltwater Country: journey to the songlines of Carpentaria.* Sydney: Allen & Unwin, 2010.

Cooke, S. *Speaking the Earth's Languages: a theory for Australian-Chilean postcolonial poetics.* Amsterdam & New York: Rodopi, 2013.

Deleuze, G. *Two Regimes of Madness.* Trans. Hodges, A. and Taormina, M. New York: Semiotext(e), 2006.

Joris, P. *Justifying the Margins.* Cambridge: Salt, 2009.

Keogh, R. "*Nurlu* Songs from the West Kimberley: an introduction." *Australian Aboriginal Studies.*1 (1989): 2-11.

---. "*Nurlu* Songs of the West Kimberleys." PhD Thesis. University of Sydney, 1990.

Muecke, S. *Butcher Joe.* dOCUMENTA (13) N°054 Ostfilden: Hatje Cantz, 2011.

Muecke, S., and Roe, P. "Words from the Other Side." *Social Alternatives* 9.4 (1991): 27-9.

Rothenberg, J. *Pre-Faces & Other Writings.* New York: New Directions, 1981.

Strehlow, T. G. H. *Songs of Central Australia.* Sydney: Angus & Robertson, 1971.

Turpin, M. "The Poetics of Central Australian Song." *Australian Aboriginal Studies.* 2 (2007): 100-15.

Synopsis

PART ONE

Verse 1
The spirits of George Dyuŋgayan and his father, Bulu, emerge from *Wanydyal*, a waterhole to the east of the Roebuck Plains. Bulu's spirit resides in Wanydyal, and from here all the songs and dances of the series emanate. The group contemplate which direction to travel.

Verse 2
The pair don't travel far because they see a flock of snipes flying towards them. As they get closer, however, Dyuŋgayan realises that the snipes are actually *rai* (ancestral spirits). The rai keep approaching at great speed, and veer away just in time to avoid colliding with Bulu and Dyuŋgayan; as they turn away they show their bellies like birds in flight.

Verse 3
The two men travel with the rai inland towards *Garrmurlgabu*, a few kilometres east of Dampier Downs Homestead, where white ochre for body decoration is abundant. The group don't stop here, but continue on to the north east.

Verse 4
They near *Balgandyirr*, a strip of gravel country stretching eastwards from Yeeda Station and the Fitzroy River for about sixty five kilometres. Before arriving at Balgandyirr they change direction for the west.

Verse 5
The group sees a flock of pelicans. The flock is in a single line, but the pelicans' heads are sticking out in all directions.

Verse 6
They can see *Malarra* (Mount Clarkson) in the distance.

Verse 7
They decide to head back towards *Maladya* (home), which appears smokey in the distance. Verse 7 is the *lirrga* (cue) for the dance in Verse 8.

Verse 8
The group return to Wanydyal, where a rainbow serpent causes a rainbow to appear in the sky. They are exhausted from their journey so their footsteps become slower and slower. Verse 8 is a *wirdu nurlu* ('big nurlu'), involving dancing and the donning of special headgear.

PART TWO

Verse 9
This verse commemorates a comet which passed by without incident. It is the lirrga for Verse 10.

Verse 10
Along with the comet, a crescent moon appears in the distant sky. A dance accompanies this verse.

Verse 11
Verse 11 describes a rainstorm seen in the sky to the south of Roebuck Plains.

Verse 12
A group of rai are painted up for a corroboree, but Dyuŋgayan can't see them properly because they are a long way away. This is the lirrga for Verse 13.

Verse 13

The rai come out and start dancing, kicking up huge amounts of dust. A dance accompanies this verse.

Verse 14

Two water snakes (rainbow serpents) appear in the sky to the north; their 'foreheads' shine in the sun. It is likely that this verse was given to Dyungayan by other men.

Verse 15

Verse 15 commemorates the appearance of a *wudya* (dangerous cloud), which came to the sheep camp in about 1920. The wudya passed by the camp but caused deaths at several stations on the Fitzroy River to the east.

Verse 16

Bulu's rai give sanction for all nurlu songs and dances to be made 'open' (public). Verse 16 stresses that the *Bulu* line is for everyone, confirming its political importance as a mode of cultural interplay between different groups in the West Kimberley.

Verse 17

The meaning of this final verse is unclear. Dyungayan refers to *wilany*, a horse-shaped cloud, continuing the presence of cloud formations throughout the songpoems.

Bulu
PART ONE

Verse 1

wanydyalmirri yiŋanydyina

mindi yarrabanydyina

wanydyal-   mirri yi-ŋa-ny-dyina
[place-name] [ø]   [modification of *yinyany*, 'he is there']

mindi yarra-ba-ny-dyina
[ø]   ['we see him']

Dyuŋgayan: wanydyalmirri yiŋanydyina that's the start from there now

Roe: mindi yarrabanydyina   think about which way we go
we wait   what's going to come out

Keogh: Bulu and his rai come out from Wanydyal and contemplate the direction they're going to travel across their country.

Cooke: they're bursting out
                    of Wanydyal
they're thinking about
                ( )
                    which way to go

from Wanydyal
                where to go
                        (   )
they're emerging
                they're thinking about

they're starting
                from Wanydyal...

Verse 2

guwararrirarri yiŋanydyina

dyidi yarrabanydyina

ŋanbalinbali yiŋanydyina

guwararrirarri   yi-ŋa-ny-dyina
[*guway*: snipe]   ['he's there']

dyid-i yarra-ba-ny- dyina
[stop]   ['we see him']   [ø]

ŋanbalinbali   yi-ŋa-ny-dyina
[*ŋanbala*: 'lie on back']   ['he's there']

Roe: dyidi yarrabanydyina   they bin look   he coming too
        ŋanbalinbali yiŋanydyina   ŋanbala   he fall   down
            belly up

Keogh: According to Roe, Bulu and Dyuŋgayan were together
        when they saw what Dyuŋgayan thought to be a flock
        of snipes flying towards them. As they got closer, how-
        ever, the pair realised that actually a group of rai was
        approaching. The rai were racing towards them but,
        turning over on their bellies like birds in flight, they
        veered away just in time to avoid a collision.
            The incident took place near Wanydyal.

Keogh & Roe:

R – rai and all that lot

ah that's   he was standing up

him and the old man was standing up and these rai

come[55] (K: yeah)

but they only rai   that not bird proper [laughs]

K – what he thought they were rai did he?

R – yeah   they wanna come straight   and then they

lay over (K: ah)

ŋanbala (K: nyanbala) ŋanbala he's [*rhythmicises words*]

ŋanbalinbali yiŋanydyina

they bin come straight you know straight for these two

K – and he thought that ah   Dyuŋgayan thought they

were

R – guway

K – guway but they were (R: yeah but he's only rai) they

were rai

Dyuŋgayan & Keogh:

guway (K: snipe) you know im? (K: snipe bird)

yeah   walk longa salt water   that one

longa sand pits (K: sand beds) you know all they go sand

pits

Cooke: a flock of snipes

flying toward us

wait! they're rai

fast approaching

we nearly collide

their bellies like birds'

wait! they're flying

belly-up

---

55 Keogh: the 'old man' refers to Bulu.

46

becoming rai
               racing through sky
flying toward us
              from far away

birds becoming rai
                    no more distance
nearly on top of us
               watch out!
the snipes are
             flying toward us

we watch snipe become rai
                      flying belly up…

Verse 3

mawulaŋana galydyi/galdyiriyana/ŋana

guwarrawarra

dirrin yinmamayana

mawulaŋana   galydyi/galdyiriyana/ŋana
[clay plan near Geegully Creek] [white ochre/snake]

guwarrawarra
[ø]

dirrin   yinmamayana
[right through] [he made]

Butcher Joe: snake
dyurru yimana mawula galdyiri dyurru[56]
in Mawula that one in Dyirrgali side
Mandigarrgabu   Mawula
and galdyiri bilong to marduwarra[57]
snake name galdyiri   he's there
bilong yuŋurrugu[58]
yuŋurrugu all that (Dyuŋgayan: bilong yuŋurrugu)

Keogh: Butcher Joe's interpretation centres on the understanding
of *galdyiri* as a tree snake found in Pandanus palms.
He says the snake belongs in the river, and associates it
with watersnake mythology. Dyuŋgayan confirms this
association.

Roe: galydyi dat one Garrmurlgabu
country name Garrmurlgabu
galydyi they bin see im
but they pass   they pass

---

56 Butcher Joe: "The snake went to Mawula   galdyiri snake".
57 Butcher Joe: 'marduwarra' is river.
58 Butcher Joe: 'yunjurrugu' is water snake.

rai   with that old man too   all travelling[59]

Keogh: For Paddy Roe, galydyi is white ochre. *Galydyi* is
abundant at Garrmurl. Indeed, *galydyi* is also known as
garrmurl.[60] *Galydyi*/garrmurl is used for *bandirr* (body
painting) in ceremonies and *ramu* (etchings) on wooden
artefacts.

Keogh & Roe:

K – so what's that one?
R – that's the galydyi
   galydyi dat one   Garrmurlgabu
   galydyi dat one
   galydyi then bin see im
   but he not   he not snake   galdyiri
   he not snake   that's the galydyi
K – what's galydyi then?
R – galydyi is white paint...
   not galdyiri snake   he got im wrong in this tape[61]

Keogh: For Butcher Joe, the text is about a snake associated
with the watersnake myth. Paddy Roe, on the other
hand, described how Bulu's group were travelling near a
place called Garrmurlgabu where white ochre can be
found.

Dyuŋgayan & Keogh:

D – and this one we look im, we look im for im for white
   white thing   longa ground   white [*sings Verse 3*]
K – galydyi
D – that galydyi that one wipe out you know
   we paint im   galydyi

---

59 Keogh: 'that old man' is Bulu.
60 According to Kim Ackerman, Keogh might be stating the obvious here:
galydyi would be known as garrmurl *because* of the place it comes from.
61 Keogh: 'he' refers to Butcher Joe.

Keogh: Dyuŋgayan's interpretation suggests that he and the group were travelling in an area of white ochre. While he confirms Roe's interpretation, he also confirms Butcher Joe's statement about the song's relationship to watersnake mythology.

Cooke:[62] they're travelling to Mawula

past the white ochre

(   )

passing through

they didn't stop making

galdyiri travelling

to Mawula

(   )

didn't stop

didn't stop making they're

passing the white ochre place

galdyiri

(   )

going right through

making them

making them they're

travelling

to Mawula

making the white ochre...

---

62 I have used 'galdyiri' here, despite the uncertainty about whether the group is after white ochre ('galydyi'), or if the song is in fact about the water snake ('galdyiri'). Interestingly, snake feces are usually white, so the discrepancy in interpretation diminishes if we consider that perhaps galdyiri was *responsible* for galydyi.

Verse 4

dyularralarra

larra yindina

balgandyirr ŋamaŋarinydyinayana

dyularralarra
[*dyularra*: white gum]

larra   yin-di-na
['to dodge behind something']   ['he did']

balgandyirr   ŋa-ma-ŋari-nydyi-na-yana
[place name]   ['I left something behind']

Keogh: Balgandyirr is a strip of gravel country in Nyigina
             territory. It stretches from from Yeeda Station and the
             Fitzroy River in the west to the Great North Highway
             in the east. Dyularra can be found growing on ridges
             throughout this country.

Roe: larra yindina   he turned back
             balgandyirr ŋamaŋarinydyinayana   I leave im that country[63]

Keogh: According to Roe, the group – Bulu, Dyuŋgayan and
             the rai – continued north-east from Garrmurlgabu
             to Balgandyirr. The group don't ever reach Balgandyirr,
             however. Instead they turn back, leaving the country
             behind for Mount Clarkson in the north-west.

---

63 Keogh: 'that country' refers to Balgandyirr.

Cooke: Balgandyirr white
                    gums white on the ridges
we see the gums
           on the ridges
                  before turning
    away leaving
          the country behind

for the mountain
           in the north-west
turning away
           from the white gums
                  on the ridges
  leaving Balgandyirr
        behind leaving
             the white gums

for the north-west
          we turn away
from that country we
can see the white gums
          on the ridges

from Balgandyirr we're turning
                  leaving
that white country behind…

Verse 5

mayarda dirrbin yiŋana

dyidurrudurruy

ŋaŋal yindina

mayarda   dirrbin   yi-ŋa-na
[pelican]   [Roe: 'very close, mixed up']   ['he is']

dyidu-   rrudurruy
['to hide behind']   [ø]

ŋaŋal   yin-di-na
[ø]   ['he did']

Keogh: According to Roe, the group are on their way from Bal gandyirr to Mount Clarkson when they see a flock of pelicans. The pelicans are flying very close together in a straight line.

Roe: *dyidurrudurruy*   in a straight line[64]
                  ŋaŋal yindina   his forehead stuck out

Keogh: dyidu-rrudurruy is 'one hiding behind the other'.
                  ŋaŋal yin-di-na is about how the heads of the pelicans were stuck out in all directions.

Roe: foreheads sticking out in all directions[65]

---

64 Keogh: 'dyidu-rrudurruy' are pelicans.
65 Ackerman believes that this verse refers to the pelicans' *beaks*, rather than their foreheads.

Cooke: beaks
                    (   )
                              sticking out
            from a straight line
                          of pelicans
                we see their heads out
                              in all directions

            (   ) of pelicans
                              flying close together
            one hiding
                    behind the (   )
            their beaks stuck out
                          all mixed up

            pelicans
                    flying close together
            (   )
                    behind one another
            we see them
                    sticking out from the line

            in all directions
                          the beaks of the pelicans…

Verse 6

malarra dyid yiyalmanayana

marrarri / barrarrri yiŋanydyina

malarra   dyid
[Roe: Mt. Clarkson / Dyuŋgayan: 'another place'] [stop]
yi-yal-ma-na-yana
[*yimana*: 'he went']

marrarri   barrar-rri
[Roe: 'can't see properly'] [Dyuŋgayan: 'sun'/'sunrise'/'day']
yi-ŋa-ny-dyina
['he was there']

Roe:	malarra dyid yiyalmanayana Mt. Clarkson he's standing up
Keogh:	According to Roe, the group travelled north-west from Balgandyirr towards Mt. Clarkson (see Verse 4), which they now see standing in the distance. But they can't see the mountain very clearly as it's still a long way away. Roe also points out that, since Mt. Clarkson is in Warrwa country, this poem emphasises the strong social and cultural connections between Warrwa and Nyigina people.
Dyuŋgayan	that a sun sun you know he come out well dat one well he got gear on too we longa Garrawin you know Garrawin now
Keogh:	On the other hand, Dyuŋgayan's reference to the sun suggests the verse occurred at sunrise. After all, the only two performances of Verse 6 that I witnessed occurred directly *after* Verses 9 & 10 (Verse 9 is about the morning star, which appears just before sunrise; Verse 10 is about the crescent moon). For Dyuŋgayan,

the verse refers to Garrawin, a ridge to the west of Mt. Clarkson. The word 'malarra' (from line 1), he says, doesn't refer to Mt. Clarkson, but to a different place. Dyuŋgayan's mention of "gear" also indicates that the song accompanies a dance.[66]

Cooke:

faint

far away Mt Clarkson

standing up

coming from the east

we look into the distance

Mt Clarkson there

standing up to greet us

the sun's rising

over us

we stop to watch it rise

at Garrawin

where the day begins

we see the sun coming up

to dance over Garrawin

faint / sun

we're far away / the day

at Mt. Clarkson / Garrawin

we stop to watch

we're watching

standing up / sun rising

Mt Clarkson / the sun's coming out

at Garrawin / in the distance

a new day / standing up...

---

66 Ackerman points out that the sun is wearing the ceremonial gear to indicate its high status, but this doesn't mean that a dance is involved. By wearing ceremonial gear, the sun makes his appearance yet more dramatic.

56

Verse 7

malanydyiŋana yiŋanydyina

buyurr yarrabanydyina

malanydyi- ŋana yi-ŋa-ny-dyina
[*maladya*: home/resting place] [ø] ['he's there']

buyurr yarra-ba-ny-dyina
['to make a haze'] ['we see him']

Keogh: Bulu's group head back towards home (maladya). From the height of Mt. Clarkson and Garrawin, the country appears hazy in the distance.[67]

Roe: maladya   home   like a country

Keogh: It appears that they are now in two different places: Mt. Clarkson and/or Garrawin. Thus, the difference between Roe and Dyuŋgayan's interpretations of Verse 6 has been maintained in Verse 7.

Verse 7 is the lirrga for the dance in Verse 8.

Cooke: we see it there
                    hazy
                           far away
            from Mt. Clarkson
                           from Garrawin
            we see home resting
                           in the distance

---

67 Ackerman points out that 'buyurr' can also refer to a smoke haze; what the group is seeing, in other words, is the smoke from their country.

our resting place

        our country

from Garrawin

        from Mt. Clarkson

we can see it now

      hazy

          in the distance

we see it there

      hazy country

         far away…

Verse 8

midinyburrurru

malaramalara yimanayana

midiny-   burrurru
[rainbow] [ø]

malara-malara yi-ma-na-yana
[ø]   [*yimana*: 'he went']

Roe: yimanayana   he slowed down

Keogh: According to Roe, Bulu's group return to their maladya, where they see a rainbow. Their journey is complete, but they're so tired that their feet drag as they walk slower and slower.

Keogh & Roe:

      R – well that's the last in the corroboree

      K – does that happen back at Wanydyal or...?

      R – might be there in Wanydyal

          or might be in maladya

          maladya you know we call im

          home   like a   country

          just like a barni too we[68]

          anybody look around for anything

          but somebody hide im away   he go back to maladya

          nobody can find im barni

---

68 Keogh: 'barni' is goanna.

Keogh: Verse 8 is the last in the series, and is called *wirdu nurlu* ('big nurlu'). It accompanies a dance, during which the dancer wears special headgear known as *waŋgararra*. Representing the rainbow that the group see on their return, the waŋgararra is also associated with a storm cloud, or *dyirrbal.*

As the owner of the dance, Dyuŋgayan was the only man who performed it until more recently, when, as Dyuŋgayan's younger brother, Roe was given performance rights. According to Roe, Bulu imbued the dance with a special power that could cause sickness.

Cooke:

slowing down
our feet dragging
we see a rainbow
stretching over (   )
our country's there
we're coming home

exhausted
dragging our feet
but our country's there
we can see (   )
beneath the rainbow
the looming storm

approaching
slowing down
feet dragging…

Bulu
PART TWO

Verse 9

larndyimirri yiŋanydyina

murda / buyurr yarrabanydyina

larn- dyimirri   yi-ŋa-ny-dyina
[star] [ø]   ['he's there']

murda   buyurr
[Roe: 'nothing'] [Dyuŋgayan: 'to make a haze']
yarra-ba-ny-dyina
['we see him']

Roe: murda yarrabanydyina   we bin go look im nothing

Keogh: According to Roe, this verse commemorates the appear-
          ance of a comet which passed over the sheep camp.

Roe: I bin tell you that star with a tail   we bin see im
          they only bin look im   murda yarrabany
          nothing happened
          they didn't want to know what that thing is an all that
              you know
          they only just seen it   murda yarrabany he pass
          that's the first time we seen it
          everybody seen it
          so he made a corroboree out of that too [*laughs*]

Keogh: Roe doesn't include Verse 9 in the original journey,
          because for him the verse commemorates the appearance
          of a comet in real life.

Dyuŋgayan & Keogh:
>K – what's that one about   larn
>D – larn
>K – star?
>D – you know star
>>earlys
>>earlys early time you know he come out

Keogh:
According to Dyuŋgayan, however, *larn* refers to the morning star. He sang Verses 9 & 10 *before* Verse 6, which suggests that he included it in the original journey with Bulu (Verses 1-8).

He didn't comment on this, but we can surmise his reasoning. Verse 6 describes the sunrise; therefore, by singing about the morning star (Verse 9) before the sunrise (Verse 6), Dyuŋgayan is performing the verses in chronological order.

Verse 9 is the lirrga for Verse 10.

Cooke:
in the hazy light of dawn
in the (   )
we see the first star
burning a track

across the sky
in the (   )
the comet burns a track
in dawn's light

we see it at dawn
in the sky above…

Verse 10

girridinydyimirri yiŋanydyina

burarrirarri yiŋanydyina

girridiny-dyimirri yi-ŋa-ny-dyina
[moon]　[ø]　　['he's there']

burarrirarri　yi-ŋa-ny-dyina
[*burarr.* dim]　['he's there']

Keogh:　　According to Roe, this verse describes how people saw
the new moon in the sky at the time of the comet's
appearance (Verse 9). Like the comet, the crescent moon
appeared from a long way away. The poem, says Roe,
refers to the fact that "we can just see the moon".

　　　　　　The song accompanies a dance, during which
waŋgararra (special headgear) is worn. The headgear
resembles the shape of a crescent moon.

Dyuŋgayan:　dancing one now
that one　　that the moon

Keogh:　　For Dyuŋgayan, however, the song refers only to the
moon and its accompanying dance. Of course, this is
understandable given the differences between Roe's and
Dyuŋgayan's interpretations of Verse 9.

Cooke:　　the moon's slimmest lip in the sky
we dance below the moon's crescent

we dance with the moon
its slim crescent like the path of a comet

across the sky...

Verse 11

milydyidawurruy

dyalbirrimbirrai

ŋarany ŋarany yinydyarrgana

milydyidawurruy
[*milydyidawurru*: 'rainstorm from the south']

dyalbirrimbirrai
['storm building up']

ŋarany ŋarany
[*ŋarany*: a waterhole in Garadyarri country, northwest
   of La Grange]
yiny-dyarrga-na
['it stood over, it waited, it hung over']

Roe: dyalbirrimbirrai   cloud all heap up
      ŋarany ŋarany yinydyarrgana   it's raining in Ɖarany

Keogh: According to Roe, Verse 11 describes how it rained at
        Ɖarany, a waterhole near Dampier Downs Station.
        Dyuŋgayan could tell it was raining, says Roe, because
        he could see the clouds building up to the south of the
        Roebuck Plains.

Roe: rain from this way[69]
      milydyidawurru we call im rain
      anytime cloud come we call im milydyidawurru
      [*rhythmicises words*] milydyidawurruy dyalbirrimbirrai
      ah he   making up you know dyalbirrimbirri
      rain they bin see im   from long way too

---

69 Keogh: the rain came from the south.

Keogh: Dyuŋgayan stated that the verse refers only to the clouds, and not to any rainfall. However, on another occasion he seemed to contradict this interpretation.

Dyuŋgayan: wila I look im all the rain[70]

Keogh: Verse 11 accompanies a dance, but neither Roe nor Dyuŋgayan could remember the lirrga.

Cooke: it's a rainstorm from the south
                                    all that rain
          the storm's building up
                            clouds heaping up
          hanging over Ɖarany
                        raining in that country

          rainstorm in the south
                      over the waterhole
                          in Garadyarri country

          all that rain
                    storm growing
          standing over Ɖarany
                        waiting there

          in the south
                    the storm's building
          the clouds are growing
          the storm's hanging
                        over Ɖarany
                            it's raining on the waterhole

          in the south
                    the storm's building up...

---

70 Keogh: 'wila' is water/rain

Verse 12

bandirr yarrabanydyina

burarri yiŋanydyina

dyalal yindinayana

bandirr   yarra-ba-ny-dyina
[body designs] ['we see him']

burarr-i yi-ŋa-ny-dyina
[dim]   ['he's there']

dyalal yin-di-na-yana
[ø]   ['he did']

Roe: bandirr yarrabanydyina   we seen bandirr
               burarri   can't see proper   long way
               dyalal yindinayana   he come out from dark

Keogh: According to Roe, a group of rai were painted up with
             body designs in preparation for corroboree. They used
             the white ochre from Verse 3 (galydyi). In his dream,
             Dyuŋgayan saw them emerge from the dark, but they
             didn't come close so he couldn't see them clearly.
                Verse 12 is the lirrga for Verse 13.

Roe: that one   something bin come out bandirr
               bandirr bilongu corroboree you know bandirr
               dyalal yindina he come out   from dark   you know
                    other side
               he come out in open
               burarr yiŋanydyina means   oh
               burarr   he stop long way   can't see im proper you
                   know burarr
               he just come out and he can only just see im that bandirr
               rai bin come out dancing   in dream

Cooke: something's emerging
                          from the other side
          something's coming out
                          into the open
          but it's dark
                          their faint white ochre lines

          they're painted up
                          dancing
          slowly emerging
                          in the dim light
          can't see them properly
                          dancing far away

          can barely make them out
                          the dancing rai
          dancing white ochre
                          in the open
          far away
                          the faint forms of a dream

          the rai emerging
                          ready for corroboree...

Verse 13

dadyiwurrurruy

dyunbarambara

ganal yimbanydyinayana

dadyi-wurrurruy
[ø]   ['large group of people']

dyunbarambara
[*dyunbara*: dust cloud]

ganal yim-ba-ny-dyina-yana
[ø]   [*yimbanydyina*: 'he sees him']

Roe: ganal yimbanydyinayana   he come to nothing[71]

Keogh & Roe:
          R – he come out now this fella
          [*rhythmicises words*] dadyiwurrurruy
          dyunbarambara
          dyunbarambara means he bring dust you know
          with his foot
          he come to nothing
          but he bin dust coming out dyunbarambara
          ganal yimbanydyina and he come to nothing
          when he's high up   wind blow im away you know
          you can't see any more dust
          K – so what's that dadyiwurrurruy   wurrurruy?
          R – dadyiwurrurruy that's them people coming out the[72]
          for dance   they're dancing dadyiwurrurruy
          wurrurru yiŋan   like big mob coming
          dadyi nothing   to make that corroboree

---

71 Keogh: 'he' refers to the dust.
72 Keogh: 'them people' are rai.

Keogh: According to Roe, in this verse the rai from Verse 12
           come out in full view and begin to dance. As they stamp
           the ground, clouds of dust rise up from their feet. The
           wind blows the dust away, however, so it comes to
           nothing.

Butcher Joe & Dyuŋgayan:
                D – this one nurlu I bin get im long time ago
                     when I was a young   young fella
                B – that old man name Bulu
                     that from Wanydyal
                     an he sing for   sing an dance
                     that one now dadyiwurrurru
                     he make dust
                     one time we come from Beagle Bay run to that
                          place there[73]
                     somebody dancing there
                     we look he dancing
                     marlu ginya murda he gone[74]
                D – well that one now

Keogh: According to Butcher Joe, however, it isn't the rai who
           appear, but Bulu *himself*. Bulu is dancing.
                Butcher Joe links the verse to an historical event in
           which a group of people were travelling from Beagle
           Bay. They saw a lot of dust caused by somebody
           dancing. The dancer was Bulu, but when they looked
           closer he had gone.
                Dyuŋgayan confirmed Butcher Joe's explanation.

---

73 Keogh: 'that place there' might be the Roebuck Plains.
74 Butcher Joe: "'marlu ginya murda   not him   nothing   he's gone'".

Cooke: that big mob coming
                              they're dancing
                                        they see dancing
          that big dust cloud
                              they're making corroboree
          that big dust cloud
                              somebody's dancing

          they're dancing
                    they see him dancing
                              that mob travelling
          their big corroboree
                    that dust cloud
          the wind blows
                blows
                    carries the dust away

          they see him dancing
                    that big travelling mob
                              they're dancing
          he's kicking up dust
                    clouds of dust
          the wind blows
                he's gone
                    the dust's blown away

          that big mob
                they're dancing
                    they see him dancing...

Verse 14

yalgudyan gudyarra yiŋanydyina ŋuŋgu

yawan baliny baliny yiŋanydyina nyunygu

yalgu-dyan   gudyarra yi-ŋa-ny-dyina
[*yalgu:* 'standing'] [two]   ['he 's there']
ŋuŋgu
[Roe: 'open eye']

yawan   baliny baliny
[north] [Roe: 'shiny forehead']

Dyuŋgayan & Keogh:

     D – we on top now   mipella[75]
        an we on top too
     K – galbu[76]
     D – galbu

Keogh: During my first session with Dyuŋgayan, he talked of how he, along with Bulu and the rai, were above the ground.

Keogh & Roe:

     R – that's the snake proper   yuŋurrugu
        two pella bin get up
        his one get up [*indicates forehead*] baliny baliny
     K– oh forehead
     R – forehead   yawan

---

75 Keogh: 'mipella' refers to 'us' (without the listener).
76 Keogh: 'galbu' is [to be] above something.

Keogh: According to Roe, Bulu and Dyuŋgayan saw two
              watersnakes (yungurrugu) come down from the north.
              When the two men noticed them, the snakes were
              standing up towards the south, their 'foreheads' shining
              in the sun. At first, Dyuŋgayan didn't see them properly,
              but he opened his eyes wider and the two snakes became
              clearer to him.

Dyuŋgayan: two   two kids I look im
              he go alonga tree   two pella   small ones bout that
              high   [*indicates about three feet*]
              two pella go longa tree
              yalgu   we call yalgu
              two pella bin stand up you know

Keogh   During my second session with Dyuŋgayan, it appeared
              that the "two kids" that "go alonga tree" may be rai.

Cooke: coming down from the north
                        their foreheads gleaming
          open your eyes
                      you can see them standing

          you can see them streaking
                              across the sky
          two shining foreheads
                        heading south

          they're coming from the north…

Verse 15

burrbi yarrmanydyina yiŋanydyinaŋa

dyirrbal yiŋanayana

burr-bi	yarr-ma-ny-dyina
[*burr*: 'to wish evil on']	['we met him']
yi-ŋa-ny-dyinaŋa	
['he's there']	

dyirrbal   yi-ŋa-na-yana
[big rain cloud] [*yinjana*: 'he's there']

Keogh: According to Roe, Verse 15 commemorates the appear-
ance of an unusual cloud near a sheep camp on the Roe
buck Plains around 1920. Three maban realised the
cloud was a *wudya* (a dangerous, sickness-bearing cloud).
They went to meet the cloud, and with special powers
made sure it passed without causing them harm.

It turned out, however, that the cloud wasn't meant
for the people at the sheep camp. People living on the
Myroodah, Lulungui and Sandfly stations on the Fitz-
roy River had sent destructive lightning to a community
south of Port Headland. The wudya cloud had been
sent back in exchange. All the people at Myroodah were
killed, and some of those at Lulungui and Sandfly also
died or were stricken with sickness.

Dyuŋgayan concurs with Roe, referring to the cloud as
"sickness on top" sent somewhere from the south.

Dyuŋgayan: sickness
                sickness when I bin look im
                sickness on top come up this way
                we going inside
                sickness was   was they send im from that country[77]

Cooke: we go out to meet him
                      big evil coming up
big rain cloud full of sickness
                  flying north

they sent it north
            full of sickness
we go out
         making sure it passed by

we go out to meet
         the big evil coming up…

---

77 Keogh: 'from that country' refers to the community south of Port Hedland.

Verse 16

barril yarramanydyina

raidyimirri yimanayana

dyilabumirri

barr-   il   yarra-ma-ny-dyina
[open eyes] [ø] ['we made for him']

rai-   dyi-mirri yi-ma-na-yana
[spirits] [ø]   [*yimana*: 'he went']

dyila-   bumirri
[rain-making/waterhole] [ø]

Roe: barril yarramanydyina   we made everything open for him

Keogh: According to Roe, Bulu's rai gave sanction for all the
            songs, dances and paraphernalia of this song series to be
            made public.

Dyuŋgayan, Keogh & Nellie Ɖadyuway[78]
            K – what's that one about Dyuŋgayan?
            D – that a rai [Ɖadyuway: rai] you know?
                dyila   nurlu bilongu dyila you know   dyila[79]
            Ɖ – maladyi [D: maladyi] wila[80] [D: yeah]   Ɖarraŋgani[81]
            D – that one now Ɖarranygani
                well that one now   dyila now

---

78 Ɖadyuway is a senior law woman. According to Ackerman, her authority
is indicated by the fact that she speaks of gunydyu. It is important that a
woman is using sacred and powerful material, and that it has been sanctioned
by the spirits, because such items may be restricted from women in other
areas of the Kimberley.
79 Ackerman: 'dyila' is 'living water', and refers to a permanent spring at
which rainmaking can occur.
80 Ackerman: 'wila' is water/rain, and 'maladyi wila' refers to an increase site.
81 Keogh: 'Ɖarraŋgani' means 'in the Dreaming'.

ŋ – gunydyu wila [D: gunydyu]⁸² gunydyu wila dyila

Keogh: Dyuŋgayan and Ɖadyuway imply that Bulu is closely associated with rainmaking activity, because his spirit now dwells in a waterhole. However, it's difficult to interpret the precise meaning of their statements. It appears as if the association of the nurlu with waterholes and rainmaking places (dyila) places it in the realm of restricted material (gunydyu), which reflects the poetry's close relationship to the Dreaming.

This isn't inconsistent with Roe's interpretation, either.⁸³

Cooke: the waterhole's eye
opens wide
     for (   )
the spirits coming out

the spirits bringing (   )
making rain
opening it up
     making it for (   )

sacred spring
opening up for (   )
we can see the spirits emerge

everything opening
     open eyes…

---

82 Ackerman: 'gunydyu' are sacred ceremonial boards.
83 According to Ackerman, Verse 16 is about the songs of the sacred 'living water' being made open by the rai. When material is 'open', everyone can see it – initiated or not.

Verse 17

bandirrmirri yinyanydyina

murda yarrabanydyina

bandirr-   mirri yi-ŋa-ny-dyina
[body design] [ø]   ['he's there']

murda   yarra-ba-ny-dyina
[nothing] ['we see him']

Keogh: The second line of Verse 17 is identical to the second line of Roe's version of Verse 9 ("murda yarra-ba-ny-dyina"). Of the line in Verse 9, Roe's translation was "we bin go look im nothing".

However, Roe stated that he didn't know the meaning of Verse 17.

Dyuŋgayan & Keogh:

K – which one is that one?
D – that one bandirrmirri
wilany we look im you know rain
cloud you know cloud
murda yarrabany we say[84]

Keogh: The meaning of this final verse is unclear. Dyuŋgayan refers to *wilany*, a horse-shoe shaped rain cloud. There are multiple references to cloud formations throughout the *Bulu* line.[85]

---

84 Keogh: 'murda yarrabany' means 'we see nothing'.
85 According to Ackerman, the reference to 'bandirr' indicates that this verse tells of how they saw the curve of a body painting in the sky.

Cooke: cloud bent into a U
             we go to look
                                 see (   )

             we see nothing
             a bent rain cloud

             we see you…

www.ingramcontent.com/pod-product-compliance
Lightning Source LLC
Chambersburg PA
CBHW020907100426
42737CB00044B/689